Get Rid of Fear Forever

Get Rid of Fear Forever

Faith Over Fear

Anthony Reinglas

Xtreme Publishing House

Get Rid of Fear Forever
Choosing Faith Over Fear

We live in a broken world with all kinds of crazy things going on every day including national issues, businesses closing, corruption, political and local issues in our own communities as well as other pandemic issues and the knowing that the end times are upon us. It can be very hard not to live in fear because even our day-to-day lives are so uncertain. We don't know what's going to happen and many feel safe in our own surroundings. On top of these things, we have struggles in our personal lives including our jobs, finances, relationships, and all the other things that life piles on us. We can't help but get caught up in fear from time to time.

I want to tell you today that there is help and an antidote to not only the fear, but also the very issues plaguing you , and its Jesus Christ, the Lord of Lords and King of Kings.

Let this be a guide for you to fall back on in times of trouble, fear or anxiety.

Copy the scriptures, recite them if needed and most of all, get the scriptures into your heart so much so that they do not become a repetitive quote, but a core belief that replaces and dispels all fear in your life.

If you listen to even one televised news report or look out your window into what is happening in the world today, fear or anxiety may capture your thoughts and grip your heart. What is important to understand is that we do not overcome the effects of 'the news' by denying or ignoring the evil in our world, but rather by applying scriptural truth to circumstances and responding biblically. Information concerning whatever may be a cause of fear will dispel the fear.. just like light dispels darkness.

But it doesn't take a newscast to stir up fear. The enemy, Satan, wants God's children to live in constant fear and anxiety as they stockpile worries and are burdened by cares. The Bible says such temptation is "common" to mankind (1 Corinthians 10:13). Even the strongest Christ-followers can experience the temptation to fear and worry.

2 Timothy 1:7
For God gave us a spirit not of fear but of power and love and self-control.

So the first bit of information we need is an understanding that fear is not from God. He did not initiate the fear, not does He put it upon you. He gives you a spirit of Power, love and of a sound mind.

Contrary to popular opinion, fear is a decision, not a reaction.

So what did I mean when I said proper information will dispel the fear?

Let me explain it with a scenario that I heard on a Kenneth Copeland teaching years ago.

He said that a parent can tell their child to never go near the street because a car can run them over and hurt and/or kill them if they run out into the street. This is true, but it instills fear in the child, and he will always be looking for the car in the street to kill him and trying to avert that while crossing the street; this fear will remain even when he is older; alternatively, if the parent teaches a respect for traffic and advises that there is a protocol for crossing the street safely, because a vehicle can hurt or kill you if you do not apply the rules of safety; Then the child grows up with an understanding of the laws the vehicle and his own ability to make informed decisions based on a respect learned for the more powerful vehicle. In this instance, information properly provided to the child averted a fear based situation.

So it is with you and me in our walk with Christ. The world will teach and instill fear of certain situations in you. We grow up with certain predispositions to fear when we see or experience lack as a child and our parents did not handle it in a biblical manner. Another way is when we experience loss, or a tragedy, trauma or anything that has a typical tendency to produce fear in a child growing up, most grow up with a fear that drives our entire decision making process into and through adulthood. And this is because you did not have an appropriate understanding of the situation and a working biblical knowledge of what God has to say about the situation.

It is for this reason that it becomes vital to never instill fear into your children or loved ones. Rather teach an understanding that even though a tumultuous situation happened, it's not Gods will, and His Word says XY & Z concerning it. We will choose to believe and stand by this, Word rather than what we see or even feel. Now the child grows up with a growing faith rather than fear.

Isaiah 41:10

Fear not, for I am with you; be not dismayed, for I am your God; I will strengthen you, I will help you, I will uphold you with my righteous right hand.

Notice that God says to "fear not"?

Why would He say that if you did not have a choice?

In fact, We are commanded to "fear not" and live by faith in the Lord throughout the Bible.

This is mentioned 365 times in the bible, once for each day! So let us fear not the dark forces of this world and the trials we will meet, by placing our hope in the Lord, for He is king!

Many of us have heard variations of the words "fear not" or "take heart," depending on the translation we use but what does *fear not* mean? Let's take a look at the original Hebrew and Greek for some hints as to the meaning behind these words.

Yare in the Hebrew means either a fear or astonishment.

According to Strong's "יָרֵא yârê', yaw-ray'; a primitive root; to fear; morally to revere; causatively to frighten:—affright, be (make) afraid, dread(-ful), (put in) fear(-ful, -fully, -ing), (be had in) reverence(-end), × see, terrible (act, -ness, thing)."

In other words, when the Bible tells us to fear not, it means to not experience dread. Now, let's take a look at the Greek.

"Take heart" or "be of good cheer" in the New Testament comes from the Greek word *tharseo*. It means to have courage and be of good comfort. Jesus uses this phrase a number of times when he heals the sick (Matthew 9:2), and comforts his disciples (Mark 14:27).

It reminds us that no matter what our current circumstance that we have a God who has overcome the world. Because remember that Greater is He that is in you, than he that is in this world (1 John 4:4).

The best way to overcome a fear of the end of days is to be spiritually prepared for it. When you are prepared properly for something there is no anxiety over it... many have anxiety issues and you are holding the antidote! First and foremost, you must have a personal relationship with Jesus Christ in order to have eternal life (John 3:16; Romans 10:9-10). Then you can understand that only through Him can you receive forgiveness of sin and have eternity with God. If God is your Father, there's really nothing to worry about (Luke 12:32). Knowing Christ and walking in His will go a long way towards diminishing fear of any kind.

What is fear?

Let me take a minute to define fear as we understand in from a Christian perspective.

Fear is faith in reverse; it it's the reciprocal of

faith. What does that mean? Simply put, it is faith in whatever the enemy is putting in your mind.

Just as it is impossible to please God without faith (Hebrews 11:6), it is impossible to entertain or even mobilize the enemy without fear. So we see that the inverse of the scripture is also true; when you have faith in God, He moves on your behalf, and when you have fear in a situation, you open the door for the enemy to work and work in that direction.

If I am afraid of a snake biting me, then what I have is faith in its ability to hurt me rather than Gods ability to save me. My bible says in Mark 16:18 that "They shall take up serpents; and if they drink any deadly thing, it shall not hurt them; they shall lay hands on the sick, and they shall recover.", so should I fear, or have faith? (Obviously we do not take this out of context and tempt God by purposely allowing a snake to bite us.. That's just plain stupid!)

Likewise if I fear not having food on my table, if I fear famine, pestilence or food shortages and lack or poverty coming on me, then I am having faith in the worlds system to rule my life rather than the Kingdom of Gods economy. My bible says that all the earth is the Lords and the fullness thereof (Psalms 24), so will He let me starve? NO WAY!!

So remember, when fear (Which is **F**alse **E**vidence **A**ppearing **R**eal) comes you have two choices:
Forget Everything And Run
or you can
Face Everything And Rise
The choice is yours!

Times as these that we are in will be hard on everyone and they will not get easier... Jesus told us in Mathew 24 that these things must come to pass. And we as believers have a comfort in knowing that God loves us enough to care of us in every situation. Christians are told what will happen in the end, and it's encouraging and even exciting when you have an understanding of the true depth of the Love of God.

1 Thessalonians 4:13-4:18 (NIV)

But we do not want you to be uninformed, brothers, about those who are asleep, that you may not grieve as others do who have no hope.

For since we believe that Jesus died and rose again, even so, through Jesus, God will bring with him those who have fallen asleep. For this we declare to you by a word from the Lord, that we who are alive, who are left until the coming of the Lord, will not precede those who have fallen asleep.

For the Lord himself will descend from heaven with a cry of command, with the voice of an archangel, and with the sound of the trumpet of God.

And the dead in Christ will rise first. Then we who are alive, who are left, will be caught up together with them in the clouds to meet the Lord in the air, and so we will always be with the Lord.

Therefore encourage one another with these words.

Rather than fear the future, we are called to anticipate the future with joy. Why? In Christ, we will be "caught up" to meet Him and we "will always be with the Lord."

Further, Scripture says we do not need to fear Judgment Day:

1 John 4:17-18

[17] Herein is our love made perfect, that we may have boldness in the day of judgment: because as he is, so are we in this world.

[18] There is no fear in love; but perfect love casteth out fear: because fear hath torment. He that feareth is not made perfect in love

The apostle Peter reveals that, even if our future holds suffering, we need not fear:

1 Peter 3:14

But and if ye suffer for righteousness' sake, happy are ye: and be not afraid of their terror, neither be troubled;

Peter and many other early believers endured much hardship and even death because of their faith in Christ. Suffering is not to be feared; it is a blessing when it is borne for the name of Jesus.

Those who do not know Christ do not have the

promise of peace for the future. For them, there is a real concern because they have not settled the issue of where they will spend eternity. Those who do know Christ do not fear the end of days. Instead, we strive to live a life worthy of our calling, live with confidence, suffer patiently, anticipate Jesus' return, and rest in the knowledge that our times are in His hands

Psalm 31:15

My times are in thy hand: deliver me from the hand of mine enemies, and from them that persecute me.

Don't borrow future worries.

Mathew 6:25-34

25 "Therefore I say to you, do not worry about your life, what you will eat or what you will drink; nor about your body, what you will put on. Is not life more than food and the body more than clothing?

26 Look at the birds of the air, for they neither sow nor reap nor gather into barns; yet your

heavenly Father feeds them. Are you not of more value than they?

²⁷ Which of you by worrying can add one cubit to his stature?

²⁸ So why do you worry about clothing? Consider the lilies of the field, how they grow: they neither toil nor spin;

²⁹ and yet I say to you that even Solomon in all his glory was not arrayed like one of these.

³⁰ Now if God so clothes the grass of the field, which today is, and tomorrow is thrown into the oven, *will He* not much more *clothe* you, O you of little faith?

³¹ "Therefore do not worry, saying, 'What shall we eat?' or 'What shall we drink?' or 'What shall we wear?'

³² For after all these things the Gentiles seek. For your heavenly Father knows that you need all these things.

³³ But seek first the kingdom of God and His righteousness, and all these things shall be added to you.

³⁴ Therefore do not worry about tomorrow, for tomorrow will worry about its own things. Sufficient for the day *is* its own trouble.

There is SO MUCH in these verses that I would like to share, but I will stick to the basics and theme of this book.

Take a look at what Jesus is saying here... Let me paraphrase it for you as we break it down...
Do not worry about your life, what you will eat or what you will drink; nor about your body, what you will put on. Is not life more than food and the body more than clothing? Take a good look at Gods smaller creations such as the birds, they do not sow or reap nor do they store away, prep for disaster, accumulate food for a rainy day and yet your heavenly Father feeds them every day!.. Are you not of more value than they? Will the worrying about these things bring you any gain?

If God cares about the flowers and the grass that is here today and then cut and thrown into the field tomorrow, how much more do you think He cares for you? To remain if fear and anxiety over these things is to disregard faith. So don't worry about what you'll wear, what you are going to eat and where you'll eat because God watches out for his own (you). Worldly people who do not know God worry about these things because they have no faith and do not understand Gods Love.

So seek first the Kingdom of God, and His righteousness, and then because you put God (the King) and His Kingdom first He will take care of all these things and more!

The more you worry about things that God has under control, the more you tie His hands, **so let go and let God!**

The bible says to think upon things that are of a good report (Phil 4:8) and stop thinking upon things that breed fear.. Essentially, its garbage in-garbage out.

To help you with good nourishing food for your spirit to rid yourself of fear and anxiety, I have placed scriptures below for your daily mediation.. Underline the ones that feed you and recite them daily until they become real to you and alive in your spirit...

1. **1 John 4:18** *Such love has no fear, because perfect love expels all fear. If we are afraid, it is for fear of punishment and this shows that we have not fully experienced his perfect love.*

2. **Isaiah 43:1** *But now thus says the Lord, he who created you, O Jacob, he who formed you, O Israel: "Fear not, for I have redeemed you; I have called you by name, you are mine.*

3. **Isaiah 41:13** *For I, the Lord your God, hold your right hand; it is I who say to you, "Fear not, I am the one who helps you.*

4. **2 Timothy 1:7** *For God gave us a spirit not of fear but of power and love and self-control.*

5. **Deuteronomy 31:6** *Be strong and courageous. Do not fear or be in dread of them, for it is the Lord your God who goes with you. He will not leave you or forsake you.*

6. **Joshua 1:9** *Have I not commanded you? Be strong and courageous. Do not be frightened, and do not be dismayed, for the Lord your God is with you wherever you go.*

7. **Psalm 34:4** *I sought the Lord, and he answered me and delivered me from all my fears.* ~

8. **Psalm 27:1** *The Lord is my light and my*

salvation; whom shall I fear? The Lord is the stronghold of my life; of whom shall I be afraid?

9. **Psalm 23:4** *Even though I walk through the valley of the shadow of death, I will fear no evil, for you are with me; your rod and your staff, they comfort me.*

10. **Philippians 4:6-7** *Do not be anxious about anything, but in everything by prayer and supplication with thanksgiving let your requests be made known to God. And the peace of God, which surpasses all understanding, will guard your hearts and your minds in Christ Jesus.*

11. **John 14:27** *Peace I leave with you; my peace I give to you. Not as the world gives do I give to you. Let not your hearts be troubled, neither let them be afraid.*

12. **Philippians 4:13** *I can do all things through him who strengthens me.*

13. **Exodus 15:2** *The Lord is my strength and my song, and he has become my salvation; this is my God, and I will praise him, my father's God, and I will exalt him.*

14. **Ephesians 6:10** *Finally, be strong in the Lord and in the strength of his might.*

15. **1 Corinthians 10:13** *No temptation has overtaken you that is not common to man. God is faithful, and he will not let you be tempted beyond your ability, but with the temptation he will also provide the way of escape, that you may be able to endure it.*

16. **1 Chronicles 16:11** *Seek the Lord and his strength; seek his presence continually!*

17. **Mark 11:22-24** *And Jesus answered them, "Have faith in God. Truly, I say to you, whoever says to this mountain, 'Be taken up and thrown into the sea,' and does not doubt in his heart, but believes that what he says will come to pass, it will be done for him. Therefore I tell you, whatever you ask in prayer, believe that you have received it, and it will be yours.*

18. **Hebrews 11:6** *And without faith it is impossible to please him, for whoever would draw near to God must believe that he exists and that he rewards those who seek him.*

19. **James 2:19** *You believe that God is one; you do well. Even the demons believe—and shudder!*

20. **Luke 1:37** *For nothing will be impossible with God.*

21. **Proverbs 3:5-6** *Trust in the Lord with all your heart, and do not lean on your own understanding. In all your ways acknowledge him, and he will make straight your paths.*

22. **1 John 4:18** *There is no fear in love, but perfect love casts out fear. For fear has to do with punishment, and whoever fears has not been perfected in love.*

23. **Isaiah 41:10** So do not fear, for I am with you; do not be dismayed, for I am your God. I will strengthen you and help you; I will uphold you with my righteous right hand.

24. **Psalm 56:3** When I am afraid, I put my trust in you.

25. **Philippians 4:6-7** Do not be anxious about anything, but in every situation, by prayer and petition, with thanksgiving, present your requests to God. And the peace of God, which transcends all understanding, will guard your hearts and your minds in Christ Jesus.

26. **John 14:27** Peace is what I leave with you; it is my own peace that I give you. I do not

give it as the world does. Do not be worried
and upset; do not be afraid.

27. **2 Timothy 1:7** For God has not given us a
spirit of fear, but of power and of love and
of a sound mind.

28. **1 John 4:18** There is no fear in love. But
perfect love drives out fear, because fear has
to do with punishment. The one who fears
is not made perfect in love.

29. **Psalm 94:19** When anxiety was great within
me, your consolation brought joy to my
soul.

30. **Isaiah 43:1** But now, this is what the Lord
says...Fear not, for I have redeemed you; I
have summoned you by name; you are mine.

31. **Proverbs 12:25** An anxious heart weighs a
man down, but a kind word cheers him up.

32. **Psalm 23:4** Even though I walk through the
valley of the shadow of death, I will fear no
evil, for you are with me; your rod and your
staff, they comfort me.

33. **Joshua 1:9** Have I not commanded you? Be
strong and courageous. Do not be terrified;
do not be discouraged, for the Lord your
God will be with you wherever you go.

34. **Matthew 6:34** Therefore do not worry about tomorrow, for tomorrow will worry about itself. Each day has enough trouble of its own.

35. **1 Peter 5:6-7** Humble yourselves, then, under God's mighty hand, so that he will lift you up in his own good time. Leave all your worries with him, because he cares for you.

36. **Isaiah 35:4** Tell everyone who is discouraged, Be strong and don't be afraid! God is coming to your rescue...

37. **Luke 12:22-26** Do not worry about your life, what you will eat; or about your body, what you will wear. Life is more than food, and the body more than clothes. Consider the ravens: They do not sow or reap, they have no storeroom or barn; yet God feeds them. And how much more valuable you are than birds! Who of you by worrying can add a single hour to his life? Since you cannot do this very little thing, why do you worry about the rest?

38. **Psalm 27:1** The Lord is my light and my salvation—whom shall I fear? The Lord is

the stronghold of my life—of whom shall I be afraid?

39. **Psalm 55:22** Cast your cares on the Lord and he will sustain you; he will never let the righteous fall.

40. **Mark 6:50** Immediately he spoke to them and said, 'Take courage! It is I. Don't be afraid.'

41. **Deuteronomy 31:6** Be strong and courageous. Do not be afraid or terrified because of them, for the Lord your God goes with you; he will never leave you nor forsake you.

42. **Isaiah 41:13-14** 'For I am the Lord, your God, who takes hold of your right hand and says to you, Do not fear; I will help you. Do not be afraid, for I myself will help you,' declares the Lord, your Redeemer, the Holy One of Israel.

43. **Psalm 46:1** God is our refuge and strength, an ever-present help in trouble.

44. **Psalm 118:6-7** The Lord is with me; I will not be afraid. What can man do to me? The Lord is with me; he is my helper.

45. **Proverbs 29:25** Fear of man will prove to

be a snare, but whoever trusts in the Lord is kept safe.

46. **Mark 4:39-40** He got up, rebuked the wind and said to the waves, "Quiet! Be still!" Then the wind died down and it was completely calm. He said to his disciples, "Why are you so afraid? Do you still have no faith?

47. **Psalm 34:7** The angel of the Lord encamps around those who fear him, and he delivers them.

48. **1 Peter 3:14** But even if you suffer for doing what is right, God will reward you for it. So don't worry or be afraid of their threats.

49. **Psalm 34:4** I prayed to the Lord, and he answered me. He freed me from all my fears.

50. **Deuteronomy 3:22** Do not be afraid of them; the Lord your God himself will fight for you.

51. **Revelation 1:17** Then he placed his right hand on me and said: 'Do not be afraid. I am the First and the Last.

52. **Mark 5:36** Jesus told him, 'Don't be afraid; just believe.

53. **Romans 8:38-39** And I am convinced that nothing can ever separate us from God's

love. Neither death nor life, neither angels nor demons, neither our fears for today nor our worries about tomorrow—not even the powers of hell can separate us from God's love.

54. **Zephaniah 3:17** The Lord your God is in your midst, A victorious warrior. He will exult over you with joy, He will be quiet in His love, He will rejoice over you with shouts of joy.

55. **Isaiah 41:10** Don't be afraid, for I am with you. Don't be discouraged, for I am your God. I will strengthen you and help you. I will hold you up with my victorious right hand.

56. **Psalm 91:1-16** He who dwells in the shelter of the Most High will rest in the shadow of the Almighty. I will say of the Lord, "He is my refuge and my fortress, my God, in whom I trust."...He will cover you with his feathers, and under his wings you will find refuge; his faithfulness will be your shield and rampart. You will not fear the terror of night, nor the arrow that flies by day, nor the pestilence that stalks in the darkness,

nor the plague that destroys at midday. A thousand may fall at your side, ten thousand at your right hand, but it will not come near you...For he will command his angels concerning you, to guard you in all your ways..."Because he loves me," says the Lord, "I will rescue him; I will protect him, for he acknowledges my name. He will call upon me, and I will answer him; I will be with him in trouble, I will deliver him and honor him...

Dear Lord,

You know that we live in a crazy and chaotic world. You also know my struggles in my daily life. When life gets to be too much, please help me come to you. Calm my thoughts and emotions and open my heart to your peace, comfort, and wisdom. Help me not to live in fear. Please reduce the feelings of fear and anxiety that plague me. Help me rest in You and trust You as I navigate through this broken world. In Your name I pray, Jesus. Amen.

If this book has blessed you, I encourage you to leave an honest review on Amazon or Google to help us and help others find it.

If you have not yet ordered a copy of my new book, *The Kingdom, the Power & the Glory: Manifesting the Kingdom of God*, get it now! This highly informative new book, will explain the Kingdom of God like never before and unlock some secrets, doors and keys to the Kingdom that will fuel and ignite your walk, mission and purpose while allowing you to live in a way that will blow people's minds!

All things for the Kingdom
Anthony Reinglas

Link to my
Amazon
author page